The Age of Dinosaurs

Meet Brachiosaurus

Written by Mark Cunningham

Illustrations by Leonello Calvetti and Luca Massini

Cavendish
Square
New York

Published in 2014 by Cavendish Square Publishing, LLC
303 Park Avenue South, Suite 1247, New York, NY 10010

First Edition

Website: cavendishsq.com

CPSIA Compliance Information: Batch #WW14CSQ

All websites were available and accurate when this book was sent to press.

Library of Congress Cataloging-in-Publication Data

Cunningham, Mark.
Meet brachiosaurus / by Mark Cunningham.
p. cm. — (The age of dinosaurs)
Includes index.
ISBN 978-1-62712-601-4 (hardcover) ISBN 978-1-62712-602-1 (paperback) ISBN 978-1-62712-603-8 (ebook)
1. Brachiosaurus — Juvenile literature. I. Cunningham, Mark. II. Title.
QE862.S3 D35 2014
567.913—dc23

Editorial Director: Dean Miller
Art Director: Jeffrey Talbot
Designer: Joseph Macri
Photo Researcher: Julie Alissi, J8 Media
Production Manager: Jennifer Ryder-Talbot
Production Editor: Andrew Coddington

Illustrations by Leonello Calvetti and Luca Massini.

The photographs in this book are used by permission and through the courtesy of: Claudia Uribe/Photodisc/Getty Images, 8; Quadell/Brachiosaurus leg bone/GNU Free Documentation License/Creative Commons Attribution-Share Alike 3.0 Unported license, 20; Ingo Schulz Image Broker/Newscom, 21.

Printed in the United States of America

CONTENTS

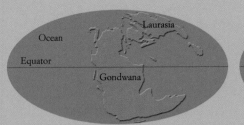

Late Triassic
227 – 206 million years ago.

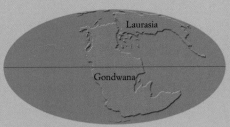

Early Jurassic
206 – 176 million years ago.

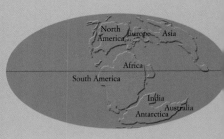

Middle Jurassic
176 – 159 million years ago.

A CHANGING WORLD

Earth's long history began 4.6 billion years ago. Dinosaurs were among the most fascinating animals from Earth's long past.

The word "dinosaur" originates from the Greek words *deinos* and *sauros*, which together mean "fearfully great lizards."

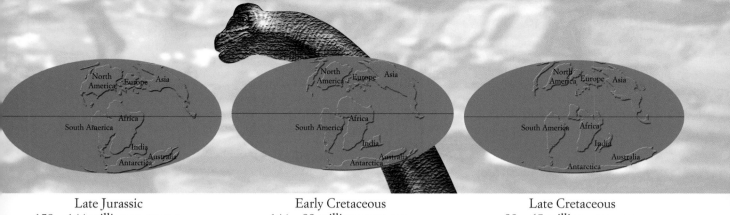

Late Jurassic	Early Cretaceous	Late Cretaceous
159 – 144 million years ago.	144 – 99 million years ago.	99 – 65 million years ago.

To understand dinosaurs we need to understand geological time, the lifetime of our planet. Earth history is divided into eras, periods, epochs, and ages. The dinosaur era, called the Mesozoic Era, is divided in three periods: Triassic, which lasted 42 million years; Jurassic, 61 million years; and Cretaceous, 79 million years. Dinosaurs ruled the world for over 160 million years.

Man never met dinosaurs. They had disappeared nearly 65 million years before man's appearance on Earth.

The dinosaur world differed from our world. The climate was warmer, the continents were different, and grass did not even exist!

5

A GIANT DINOSAUR

Brachiosaurus was a saurischian dinosaur belonging to the suborder Sauropoda that includes animals popularly known as sauropods or "brontosaurs," meaning the giant "long necks." Sauropods were herbivores who made the ground tremble under their footsteps. Brachiosaurus lived around 150 million years ago at the end of the Jurassic Period.

The head appeared small at the end of a very long and stiff neck. Unlike the neck, its tail is rather short, especially when compared to similar dinosaurs, like Diplodocus or Apatosaurus.

Brachiosaurus moved on four feet (1.2 m) and was very slow because of its enormous size. Scientists have calculated that its walking speed (of course, it was unable to run!) could not exceed 10 miles per hour (16.1 km/h) and probably the large adults moved much more slowly.

The front legs were longer than the hind legs and its back was downward sloping, instead of being horizontal like in other sauropod dinosaurs.

The adult brachiosaurs probably slept standing, because they would not be able to raise their enormous body once on the ground.

7

FINDING BRACHIOSAURUS

We know about two species: Brachiosaurus altithorax, which lived in the North American plains, and Brachiosaurus brancai, which walked on the African continent.

The brachiosaur was rare in North America, where the most common sauropods were the camarasaurs, the apatosaurs (the true "brontosaurs"), and Diplodocus. On the other side of the world, along the coastal plains of Tanzania, it would have been easier to meet this immense dinosaur.

Tanzania, Africa.

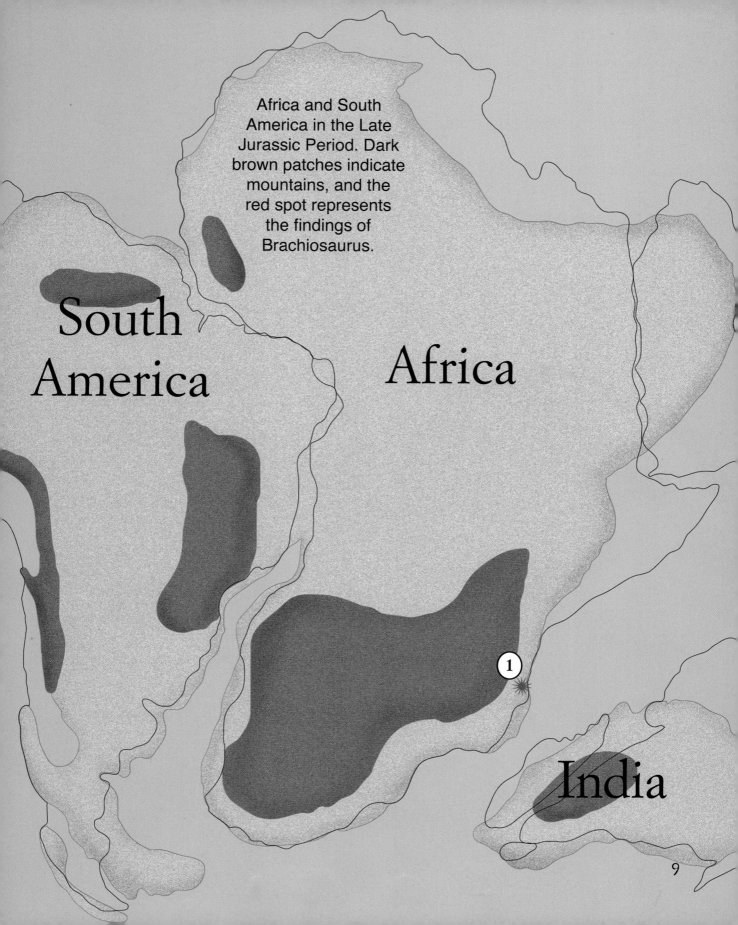

Africa and South America in the Late Jurassic Period. Dark brown patches indicate mountains, and the red spot represents the findings of Brachiosaurus.

South America

Africa

India

①

BIRTH

Brachiosaurus hatchlings came into the world from large spherical eggs that the mother laid in the sand. They had large heads with wide eyes. The young seemed to have lived in a herd with the adults, so parents may have kept watch over the nest to protect the eggs and hatchlings.

FEEDING TIME

Like an enormous giraffe, Brachiosaurus could reach high up in the trees for food. Its teeth were strong enough to tear off leaves and small branches. Younger and smaller individuals fed on lower plants and tender shoots.

Brachiosaurus swallowed food without chewing it. Like some modern birds, the Brachiosaurus would swallow stones (called gastroliths) that would sit in its stomach and help grind up food.

DRY SEASON

Brachiosaurus lived along relatively dry coastal plains that were similar to the present-day African savannah. However, plants were different from today. Grass did not yet exist and there were no flowering plants, such as palm trees.

The dry season used to follow the short rain season. Finding abundant vegetation to feed on and water to drink became a problem for the young brachiosaurs and their herd. Lack of water was a concern for all the dinosaurs of the plains. Usually they met to drink side by side around the few surviving puddles. Of course, predators, including crocodiles, were waiting in ambush for them.

BAD ENCOUNTERS

Brachiosaurus was the largest animal of its time and probably no predators dared to attack the adults. However, the young could fall prey to carnivorous dinosaurs like the agile Elaphrosaurus, which was up to 18 feet (5.5 m) long. Taking advantage of a moment of inattention while the herd was feeding on leaves up among the branches of the trees, the predators could approach the helpless young and attack them. They knew that the giant parent was extremely slow and not particularly agile.

However, the elaphrosaurs preferred to attack easier prey, like dryosaurs, because a fight with an adult brachiosaur could prove fatal.

INSIDE BRACHIOSAURUS

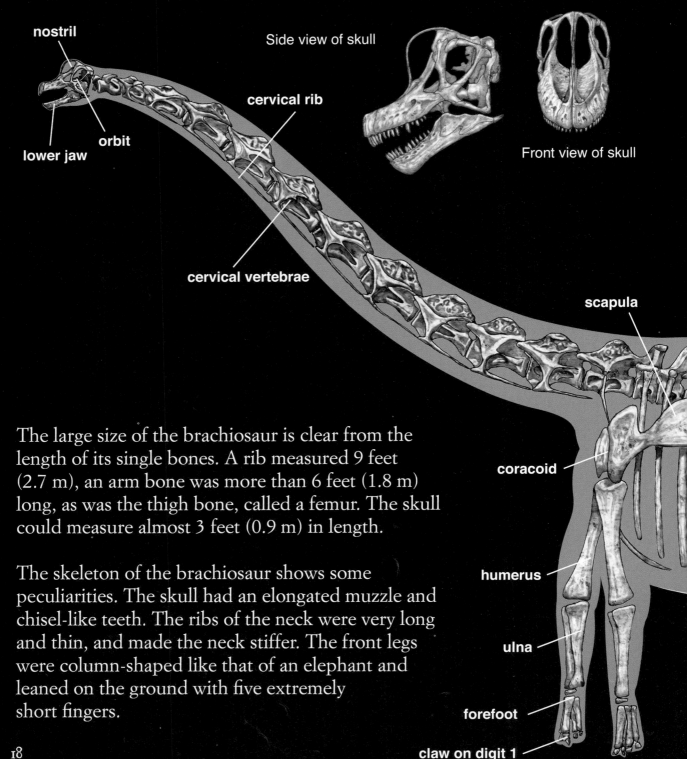

nostril

Side view of skull

cervical rib

orbit

lower jaw

Front view of skull

cervical vertebrae

scapula

coracoid

humerus

ulna

forefoot

claw on digit 1

The large size of the brachiosaur is clear from the length of its single bones. A rib measured 9 feet (2.7 m), an arm bone was more than 6 feet (1.8 m) long, as was the thigh bone, called a femur. The skull could measure almost 3 feet (0.9 m) in length.

The skeleton of the brachiosaur shows some peculiarities. The skull had an elongated muzzle and chisel-like teeth. The ribs of the neck were very long and thin, and made the neck stiffer. The front legs were column-shaped like that of an elephant and leaned on the ground with five extremely short fingers.

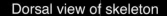
Dorsal view of skeleton

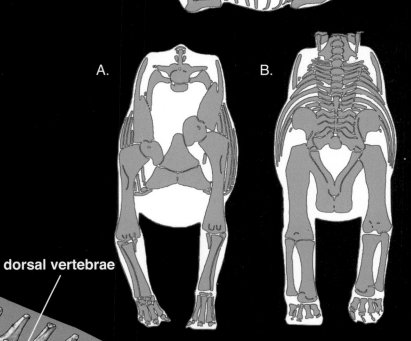
A.

B.

A. Anterior view of skeleton (without neck and skull).

B. Posterior view of skeleton (without tail).

C. Right forefoot of Brachiosaurus

D. Right hindfoot of Camarasaurus, a sauropod relatively close to Brachiosaurus.

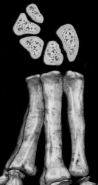
C.

D.

dorsal vertebrae

ilium

ischium

caudal vertebrae

dorsal rib

pubis

femur

tibia

fibula

hind foot

chevron

FINDING BRACHIOSAURUS FOSSILS

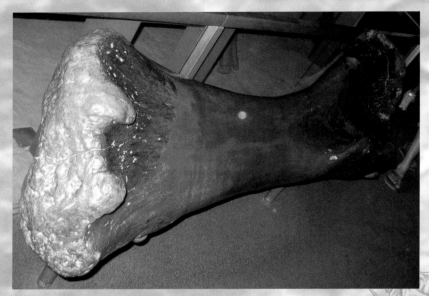

Above: Ulna of Brachiosaurus, a big sauropod.

The brachiosaurs were enormous animals. After their death, their bodies were often dismembered either by predators, or by the violent currents of flooded rivers. Only incomplete carcasses reached the bottom of rivers and lakes and were eventually covered by sediment. In some instances it seems that the animal died stuck in quicksand, and for this reason, its limbs are preserved vertically in the sediment like giant pillars.

Officially, the first skeleton of a Brachiosaurus, incomplete and without a skull, was found in 1900, in Colorado, by the paleontologist Elmer S. Riggs and his team of dinosaur researchers. In 1903, Riggs named his find Brachiosaurus (from Latin and Greek words meaning "lizard-arm"), because of the large size of the arm.

Original skeletons of brachiosaur are few; museums exhibiting one are scarce. The most famous specimen is in The Humboldt Museum of Berlin. It is the largest original mounted dinosaur skeleton in the world.

The skeleton is 74 feet (22.5 m) long and 39 feet (11.9 m) high. Its body mass has recently been estimated between 31 to 54 tons (28–49 t). The brachiosaur was decidedly a giant animal and its figure was impressive.

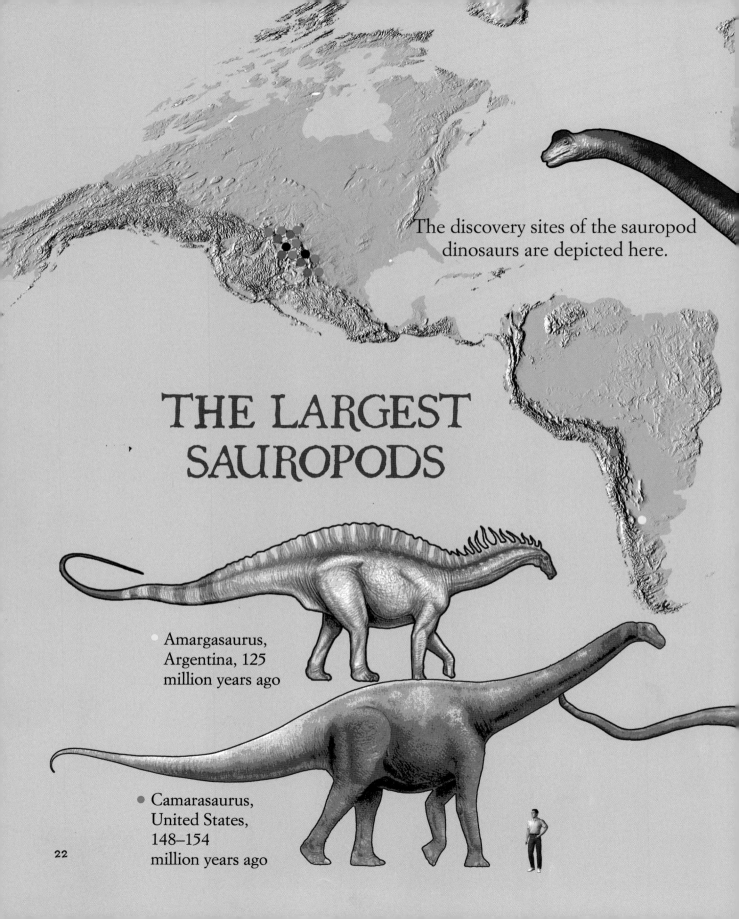

The discovery sites of the sauropod dinosaurs are depicted here.

THE LARGEST SAUROPODS

Amargasaurus, Argentina, 125 million years ago

Camarasaurus, United States, 148–154 million years ago

Sauropods were widespread all around the world for over 140 million years. They were particularly abundant and diversified in North America during the Late Jurassic Period and in South America during Cretaceous times, 125 to 70 million years ago. Rarely the length of an adult sauropod was less than 39 feet (12 m), but dwarf species existed in Europe.

• Brachiosaurus, Tanzania and United States, 145–155 million years ago

• Saltasaurus, Argentina, 70–75 million years ago

• Diplodocus, United States, 148–154 million years ago

THE GREAT EXTINCTION

Sixty-five million years ago (about 60 million years after the time of Brachiosaurus), dinosaurs became extinct. Scientists think a large meteorite hitting the earth caused this extinction. A wide crater caused by a meteorite exactly 65 million years ago has been located along the coast of Mexico. The dust suspended in the air by the impact would have obscured the sunlight for a long time, causing a drastic drop in temperature and killing many plants.

The plant-eating dinosaurs would have starved or frozen to death. Meat-eating dinosaurs would have also died without their food supply. However, some scientists believe dinosaurs did not die out completely, and that present-day chickens and other birds are, in a way, the descendants of the large dinosaurs.

A DINOSAUR'S FAMILY TREE

The oldest dinosaur fossils are 220–225 million years old and have been found all over the world.

Dinosaurs are divided into two groups. Saurischians are similar to reptiles, with the pubic bone directed forward, while the Ornithischians are like birds, with the pubic bone directed backward.

Saurischians are subdivided in two main groups: Sauropodomorphs, to which quadrupeds and vegetarians belong; and Theropods, which include bipeds and predators.

Ornithischians are subdivided into three large groups: Thyreophorans which include the quadrupeds Stegosaurians and Ankylosaurians; Ornithopods; and Marginocephalians subdivided into the bipedal Pachycephalosaurians and the mainly quadrupedal Ceratopsians.

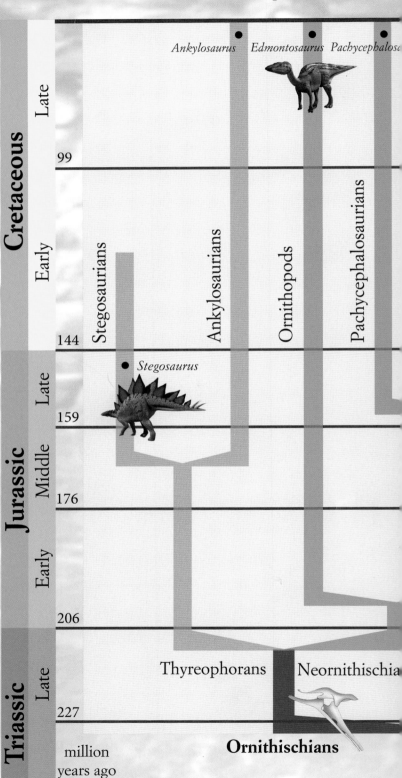

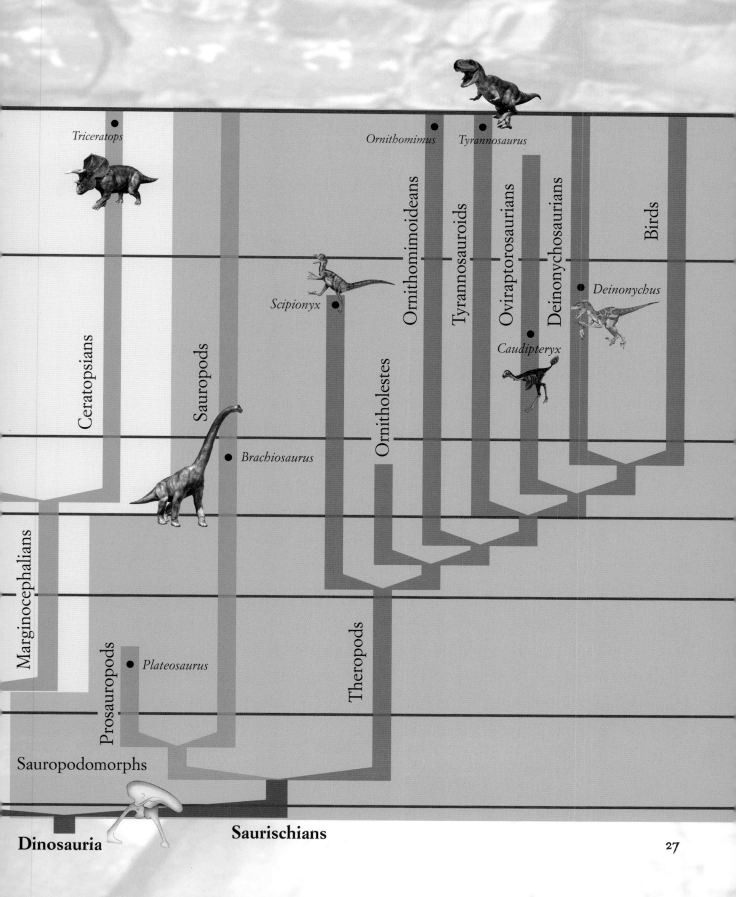

Triceratops

Ornithomimus

Tyrannosaurus

Ceratopsians

Sauropods

Ornithomimoideans

Tyrannosauroids

Oviraptorosaurians

Deinonychosaurians

Birds

Scipionyx

Deinonychus

Caudipteryx

Ornitholestes

Brachiosaurus

Marginocephalians

Theropods

Prosauropods

Plateosaurus

Sauropodomorphs

Dinosauria

Saurischians

27

A SHORT VOCABULARY OF DINOSAURS

Bipedal: pertaining to an animal moving on two feet alone, almost always those of the hind legs.

Bone: hard tissue made mainly of calcium phosphate; single element of the skeleton.

Carnivore: a meat-eating animal.

Caudal: pertaining to the tail.

Cenozoic Era (Caenozoic, Tertiary Era): the interval of geological time between 65 million years ago and present day.

Cervical: pertaining to the neck.

Claws: the fingers and toes of predator animals end with pointed and sharp nails, called claws. Those of plant-eaters end with blunt nails, called hooves.

Cretaceous Period: the interval of geological time between 144 and 65 million years ago.

Egg: a large cell enclosed in a porous shell produced by reptiles and birds to reproduce themselves.

Epoch: a division of geologic time.

Evolution: changes in the character states of organisms, species and higher ranks through time.

Feathers: outgrowth of the skin of birds and some other dinosaurs, used in flight and in providing insulation and protection of the body. They evolved from reptilian scales.

Forage: to wander in search of food.

Fossil: evidence of the life in the past. Not only bones, but footprints and trails made by animals, as well as dung, eggs, or plant resin, when fossilized, is a fossil.

Herbivore: a plant-eating animal.

Jurassic Period: the interval of geological time between 206 and 144 million years ago.

Mesozoic Era (Mesozoic, Secondary Era): the interval of the geological time between 248 and 65 million years ago.

Pack: group of predator animals acting together to capture the prey.

Paleontologist: scientists who study and reconstruct prehistoric life.

Paleozoic Era (Paleozoic, Primary Era): the interval of geological time between 570 and 248 million years ago.

Predator: an animal that preys on other animals for food.

Raptor (raptorial): a bird of prey, such as an eagle, hawk, falcon, or owl.

Rectrix (plural rectrices): any of the larger feathers in a bird's tail that are important in helping its flight direction.

Scavenger: an animal that eats dead animals.

Skeleton: a structure of animal body made of several different bones. One primary function is also to protect delicate organs such as the brain, lungs, and heart.

Skin: the external, thin layer of the animal body. Skin cannot fossilize unless it is covered by scales, feathers, or fur.

Skull: bones that protect the brain and the face.

Teeth: tough structures in the jaws used to hold, cut, and sometimes process food.

Terrestrial: living on land.

Triassic Period: the interval of geological time between 248 and 206 million years ago.

Vertebrae: the single bones of the backbone; they protect the spinal cord.

DINOSAUR WEBSITES

Dinosaur Train (pbskids.com/dinosaurtrain/): From the PBS show Dinosaur Train, you can have fun watching videos, printing out pages to color, play games, and learn lots of facts about so many dinosaurs!

The Natural History Museum (http://www.nhm.ac.uk/kids-only/dinosaurs/): Take a quiz to see how much you know about dinosaurs or a quiz to tell you what type of dinosaur you'd be! There's also a fun directory of dinosaurs, including some cool 3D views of your favorites.

Discovery Channel Dinosaur videos (http://dsc.discovery.com/video-topics/other/dinosaur-videos): Watch almost 100 videos about the life of dinosaurs!

Dinosaurs for Kids (www.kidsdinos.com): There's basic information about most dinosaur types, and you can play dinosaur games, vote for your favorite dinosaur, and learn about the study of dinosaurs, paleontology.

DinoData (www.dinodata.org): Get the latest news on dinosaur research and discoveries. This site is pretty advanced, so you may need a teacher's or parent's help to find what you're looking for.

MUSEUMS

Yale Peabody Museum of Natural History, 170 Whitney Avenue, New Haven, CT 06520-8118

American Museum Natural History, Central Park West at 79th Street, New York, NY 10024-5192

The Field Museum, 1400 So. Lake Shore Drive, Chicago, IL 60605-2496

Carnegie Museum of Natural History, 4400 Forbes Avenue, Pittsburgh, PA 15213-4080

National Museum of Natural History, the Smithsonian Institution, 10th Street and Constitution Avenue NW, Washington, DC 20560-0136

Museum of the Rockies, 600 W. Kagy Boulevard, Bozeman, MT 59717

Denver Museum of Nature and Science, 2001 Colorado Boulevard, Denver, CO 80205

Dinosaur National Monument, Highway 40, Dinosaur, CO 81610

Sam Noble Museum of Natural History, 2401 Chautauqua, Norman, OK 73072-7029

Museum of Paleontology, University of California, 1101 Valley Life Sciences Bldg., Berkeley, CA 94720-4780

Royal Tyrrell Museum of Palaeontology, Hwy 838, Drumheller, AB T0J 0Y0, Canada

INDEX

Page numbers in **boldface** are illustrations.
....